AYN RAND
FOR BEGINNERS ®

AYN RAND
FOR BEGINNERS®

by **ANDREW BERNSTEIN**
illustrations by **OWEN BROZMAN**

FOR BEGINNERS®

an imprint of Steerforth Press
Hanover, New Hampshire

For Beginners LLC
62 East Starrs Plain Road
Danbury, CT 06810 USA
www.forbeginnersbooks.com

A For Beginners® Documentary Comic Book
Copyright © 2009

Cataloging-in-Publication information is available from the Library of Congress.

ISBN # 978-1-934389-37-9 Trade

Manufactured in the United States of America

For Beginners® and Beginners Documentary Comic Books® are published
by For Beginners LLC.

First Edition

10 9 8 7 6 5 4

Contents

Chapter 1
Who Was Ayn Rand?

Ayn Rand was born in Russia in 1905. Her real name was Alyssa Rosenbaum. At the age of six, she taught herself to read. At age nine, she decided that fiction writing would be her career. She was twelve years old in 1917 when the Bolshevik Revolution began, which resulted in the Communists taking over Russia a few years later. The victory of the Communists led to the confiscation of her father's pharmacy and years of severe poverty for the Rosenbaum family.

In 1926, at the age of twenty-one, Ayn Rand escaped to the United States, the country that she loved. For approximately the first six months of her stay in America, she lived with relatives in Chicago. One of her relatives owned a movie theater there, which she visited almost daily. At this time, she worked on her English language skills by practicing the writing of screenplays. She lived in America for the rest of her life, until her death in 1982. In the United States, she changed her name to Ayn Rand, probably to protect her family, who still lived in Russia under the brutal dictator, Joseph Stalin.

Ayn Rand knew from her childhood that she wanted to write fiction, because she wanted to write stories about heroes—about strong men and women who overcame any and all obstacles to accomplish difficult goals very dear to them. Such stories would echo the trajectory of her own life—in which she came alone to a foreign country, with little knowledge of English and even less money, and overcame every challenge to become one of the great novelists in the English language.

Shortly after she arrived in America, she moved to Hollywood to pursue a screenwriting career. She rented a room at the Studio Club, which provided living quarters for young women seeking careers in the film business. (Later, Marilyn Monroe, among many other future stars, lived there.) On her second day in Hollywood, Cecil B. DeMille, one of the great film directors in movie history, spotted her at the gate of his studio and offered her a ride to the set of *King of Kings*, the biblical movie on which he was then working. Struck by this young woman with the intense, dark eyes, he gave the young Ayn Rand her first jobs in America, first as an extra and later as a script reader.

A week later, while working as an extra on the DeMille set, she met her future husband, Frank O'Connor. The shy but determined Ayn Rand felt attracted to the handsome young actor, whom she later described as having an "ideal" face. During one scene, she made sure to place herself directly in his path so that he stumbled on her foot. He apologized, the ice was broken, and, as she put it years later, "the rest is history." They were married in 1929 and remained so for fifty years, until Mr. O'Connor's death in 1979. Their marriage took place shortly before the final extension of her visa expired, and led to one of the proudest days of her life—when she became a naturalized U.S. citizen in 1931.

After DeMille closed his studio, Rand worked as a filing clerk in RKO's wardrobe department, becoming the department head within a year. At about this time, she bought her first portable typewriter and began her writing career. During her free time, she wrote screenplays and short stories, and began her first novel, *We the Living*, a semi-autobiographical tale of a young woman struggling to reach her personal goals under the Communists in the Soviet Union, which was eventually published in 1936. Before the novel's publication, she sold a screenplay, *Red Pawn*, to Universal Studios for a modest sum that was sufficient for her to quit the wardrobe department and concentrate on full-time writing.

During the 1930s, she authored a courtroom drama, which ran on Broadway for more than six months, entitled *Night of January 16th*. The play's most striking feature was that the jury was composed of volunteers from the audience—so that the story had two different endings depending on the jury's verdict.

During this period, she also wrote her novella, *Anthem*, which is generally considered her first work of great fiction. It has sold several million copies, and is widely read today in American high schools. *Anthem* tells the story of an independent young mind in a Communist-style totalitarian state of the future, where all freedom of thought and expression has been abolished. Even the language has been thoroughly collectivized: all first-person singular pronouns have been expunged; men are executed for discovering and speaking the "Unmentionable Word"—"I"; and individuals think and speak of themselves exclusively as "we."

The suppression of individual thought has plunged the society into a second dark age. The story's hero, Equality 7-2521, a Thomas Edison of his generation, reinvents the electric light. His gravest sin, however, is that he dares to think, act, and stand alone against the all-powerful state—crimes for which he is condemned to death. The story presents a powerful case for the freedom and rights of the individual against the oppressive power of the totalitarian state.

Anthem was published in England in 1938, but was not published in the United States until after World War II, in 1946. Ayn Rand subsequently claimed that intellectual opposition among American publishers to its pro-individualist, anti-collectivist theme was the main reason it was not published in the United States until after World War II.

In the late 1930s, Ayn Rand began writing the book that would establish her literary reputation and bring her popular fame: *The Fountainhead*. It tells the story of a principled and brilliant young architect who struggles against virtually all of society—including the woman he loves—to build structures in accordance with his own vision and ideals. The hero, Howard Roark, who refuses to sell his soul in any form, has become an inspiration to countless readers over the nearly seven decades since its first publication.

This 700-page novel of ideas took Ayn Rand seven years to complete. But when it was done, Rand was convinced that she had a novel that was both serious and entertaining—one with both a profound theme and an exciting story. Unfortunately for her, many publishers did not agree. One leading publisher, for example, rejected the book on the ground that it was a bad novel. Another deemed it high-grade literature, but turned it down because it was too intellectual and controversial. By 1941, twelve publishers had rejected *The Fountainhead*. Finally, the editors at Bobbs-Merrill recognized what Rand had long believed about the book: it was a serious and entertaining novel that would sell. They published it in 1943.

The book that was supposedly too intellectual for commercial success has since sold, by conservative estimate, more than 6.5 million copies. Currently, *The Fountainhead* continues to sell well over 100,000 copies per year. It has achieved the status of an American classic, and is studied widely in secondary schools across the country.

Ayn Rand began full-time work on her greatest novel, *Atlas Shrugged*, in April 1946. She worked on it for many years (she stated that she wrote every page of the 1,000-page book a minimum of five times) and was finally ready to publish it in 1957. Its main idea was to raise and answer the question: *What would happen to the world if its greatest thinkers—the scientists, philosophers, writers, artists, inventors, entrepreneurs, and industrialists—went on strike?*

For years, her working title for the book was "The Strike." Her answer to the question was that advanced civilization would collapse. In *Atlas Shrugged*, Rand composed a moral defense of capitalism, expressing a battery of related points: that an individual has the right to his own life; that he furthers his life by the use of his rational mind; and that a man's right to think and live for himself requires a system of political-economic freedom, i.e., laissez-faire capitalism.

RATIONAL THOUGHT IS MAN'S SOLE MEANS OF GAINING KNOWLEDGE.

Rand discussed the possible publication of *Atlas Shrugged* with Bennett Cerf, one of the founders of Random House. He admired her novels but told her forthrightly that he found her political philosophy abhorrent. He also proposed to her a kind of philosophical contest for her manuscript—that she should offer it to multiple publishers, see what their respective attitudes toward her philosophy were, as well as how those attitudes would affect their promotional efforts for the book, and then judge for herself who she considered the best publisher for it. Cerf's blunt honesty and literary insight appealed to Ayn Rand, and they became good friends.

Additionally, one of Cerf's associates, Donald Klopfer, understood that her book's proposed moral defense of capitalism would necessarily place her in opposition to thousands of years of the Judeo-Christian tradition in ethics—and said so. She was extremely pleased by his philosophical understanding, and answered, yes, it absolutely would. This did not frighten Klopfer or Cerf, but only made them more interested in the book. To Ayn Rand, it quickly became clear that Random House was the right publisher for *Atlas Shrugged*. And so, in 1957, the publishing giant released her greatest book.

The reviews were generally scathing. One prominent critic dismissed it as "a remarkably silly book," said it could be called a novel only by "devaluing the term," complained that its shrillness is without reprieve, and concluded that Rand was akin to the Nazis—that every page of the book commands: "To a concentration camp go!" One religious reviewer stated it was the "most immoral and destructive book he'd ever read," but took comfort in the belief that its 500,000 words could not long endure in print. A famous writer described its philosophy as "nearly perfect in its immorality." *The New York Times* proclaimed that the book was "written out of hate." *The Los Angeles Times*—not to be outdone—argued that it would be hard to find such a display of "grotesque eccentricity outside an asylum." *The New Yorker* at least maintained a sense of humor about it: commenting on a scene in which the American economy is so depressed by socialist policies that a man is witnessed pulling a plow by hand, it stated, "Even the horse, it appears, cannot survive when liberals flourish." Another witty reviewer called the 1,000-page book "longer than life and twice as preposterous." Still another, not so witty, likened *Atlas Shrugged* to Adolf Hitler's book, *Mein Kampf*.

And yet, *Atlas Shrugged* founded a movement. Rand's growing number of intellectual supporters, both inside and outside the universities, fire back that *Atlas Shrugged* is the greatest novel ever written, that its brilliant plot alone ranks it as superlative literature, and that the reviews are nonobjective smears from writers who could not distinguish an extraordinary work of art from a book that espoused ideas with which they strongly disagreed.

Ayn Rand's philosophy, which she named Objectivism, is dramatized throughout the action of *Atlas Shrugged* and is presented, as well, in numerous later works of nonfiction. She argues that rational thought, not faith or feelings, is man's sole means of gaining knowledge and advancing his life on earth; that the mind is mankind's survival instrument, and that any form of abrogating reason—religious faith, for example—is harmful to human life. She claims that reality is exclusively the world of nature—that no supernatural dimension exists—and that a rational mind is capable of understanding this world, but not altering it, by a sheer process of thought. She argues that the world is lawful, and that no amount of wishing, praying, or believing can make burning bushes speak, men live inside of whales, or virgins give birth—that such miraculous claims are worse than false: they are impossible.

Further, according to Rand, human beings are not the pitiful antiheroes depicted in serious modern literature and film—helplessly buffeted by social forces, repressed psychological conflicts, or dysfunctional families. In her novels, she presents and proclaims man as the potential hero. She shows that by means of a life devoted to reason and unflagging action based on it, human beings can reach great accomplishments, and can do so, if necessary, in opposition to powerful social forces. Individuals who remain dedicated to life-promoting advances even in the teeth of powerful antagonists can reach moral greatness or heroism.

Rand argues that something is good if it factually, or objectively, promotes human life (e.g., nutritious food, an education, political-economic freedom), whereas evil is that which harms or destroys human life (e.g., poison, ignorance, political dictatorship). So the good is based on objective fact—hence the name of Objectivism for her philosophy—not on the will of God, the wishes and beliefs of society, or the whims of individuals. The only beings who are alive, who must attain the values that further their lives, and who will perish if they do not are: *individuals*. There is no collective organism, only many individuals.

Therefore, each individual must by rational thought, hard work, and honest effort seek those values which advance his own life and happiness—for example, the education, career, and personal relationships that sustain his life and fill it with meaning.

This is the moral code of *egoism*. Human beings can flourish on earth only by achieving values—not by sacrificing or surrendering them. The code of self-sacrifice, religious or secular, is immoral. Practicing goodwill and kindness toward other human beings is morally good, and rationally egoistic individuals benefit both themselves and others many times each day by helping those they care about—their children, spouses, friends, customers, clients, students, and numerous other people with whom they have relationships. It is not difficult to benefit both the self and others—but it is impossible both to fulfill and to sacrifice the self. That is a logical impossibility akin to a round square.

The only moral political-economic system is one that recognizes an individual's right to his own life, his own mind, and the pursuit of his own happiness. A proper government exists solely to protect an individual's rights, not to violate them. The proper system of government is, therefore, laissez-faire capitalism, which protects each man's right to achieve the values his life requires by the employment of his survival instrument—his rational mind.

This is a brief summary of Ayn Rand's philosophy. But what are its details? How does Ayn Rand support and validate her theories? What kinds of examples does she present to illustrate them? Let's go deeper into her books and ideas and explore the answers to such questions.

Chapter 2
The Fountainhead

The Fountainhead was published in 1943. The story is set over a period of roughly fifteen years during the 1920s and 1930s. Its hero, Howard Roark, is a modernist architect in a society that still favors classical and Renaissance styles of design. For example, he designs skyscrapers as straight, vertical structures, not as imitations of Greek temples or Gothic cathedrals. But American society during this period was not ready for his style of building.

Therefore, Roark's designs meet intense opposition. He is expelled from college because he refuses to conform to his professors' architectural theories. Indeed, at an interview explaining the expulsion, the dean of the school tells Roark that his style of design is sheer insanity, that his attitude toward others is monstrous, and that he is a man not to be encouraged because he is dangerous. Roark is fired from a job because he will not design in the style preferred by his boss. He loses commissions because clients have never before witnessed anything akin to his revolutionary designs. In short, he struggles because of his independence, his refusal to give the public what it is used to.

Roark goes to New York City, where he works for Henry Cameron. Cameron was tremendously successful decades earlier, but has lost all popularity because of the increasingly revolutionary nature of his designs. Like Roark, he designs in accordance with his own standards and refuses to conform. Now, at sixty-nine years of age, Cameron is an embittered, alcoholic commercial failure. He is also the most brilliant architect in the world. While interviewing Roark for the job, Cameron curses, calls Roark a liar, and tells him that he's abnormal—to which Roark answers, "Probably." He tells Roark that he's insufferable, impertinent, and that twenty years earlier he would have punched Roark's face with great pleasure. Cameron proceeds to hire him on the spot, but tells Roark that he will kill him if he goes to work for another architect. From Cameron, Roark does not learn how to wine, dine, or impress people—only how to build superbly.

Roark's college classmate, Peter Keating, is his exact opposite. Keating gives the professors and then the public exactly what they desire. He lies, cheats, and flatters all his superiors to get ahead. He is a conformist. He also goes to New York City after graduation, but he works for Guy Francon. Francon is a mediocre architect but an expert social butterfly and a commercial success. He dresses beautifully, has great personal charm, and wines and dines all prospective clients. From Francon, Keating learns how to impress people, not how to build.

One example of Keating's tactics for getting ahead is his reprehensible treatment of Francon's partner, Lucius Heyer. Heyer is an old, senile non-architect who garnered a partnership solely by virtue of belonging to an aristocratic family. He is useless around the office, but stays because it makes him feel important. Francon and virtually everyone on his staff are openly contemptuous of him. But not Keating.

The aggressive social climber fawns over Heyer and deviously ingratiates himself with the old man because one never knows when having a partner's friendship—even that of a doddering old fool—might come in handy. But as Keating inexorably rises, Heyer's patronage means less and less to him. After several years, Keating desires the partnership for himself. Heyer has had a serious stroke but stubbornly refuses to retire, and thus stands in Keating's way. Secretly, Keating goes to the old man's apartment and angrily berates him, knowing that Heyer's rising blood pressure could trigger a second, fatal stroke—which it does.

After Heyer's death, Keating receives the coveted partnership. He also inherits a large sum of money from Heyer because he was the only one at the office who was consistently "nice" to the childless old man. Even through the guilt of knowing his role in causing Heyer's death, when Keating learns the terms of Heyer's will, he finds himself thinking: *How much do I get?*

Keating's methods lead him to great early success. He gets Roark to help him design, charms clients, "kisses up" to superiors, and rises in Francon's firm. Roark, on the other hand, designs several buildings, but struggles because his designs are new—in fact, revolutionary.

At one point, Roark is almost penniless and depends on a possible commission for the Manhattan Bank Building. The board likes his design but wishes to alter it to suit the public's expectations. Roark refuses to compromise the integrity of his design. As a result, he must close his office and accept a workman's job in a Connecticut granite quarry.

When Roark refuses the commission, a member of the board, knowing the dire state of Roark's finances, calls him fanatical and selfless. Roark is incredulous. Tucking his drawings to his side, he replies that his action was the most selfish thing that the members of the board have ever seen a man do. He uses the term "selfish" in a positive sense, not in the conventional negative sense. He means that the board has just witnessed a man being true to himself, his values, and his highest love by refusing to surrender what is most important to him—the integrity of his design—for that which is much less important to him—money and recognition.

At the quarry, Roark meets Dominique Francon, the daughter of architect Guy Francon. She aggressively pursues him, deliberately scratching a marble fireplace to lure him to repair it—and then, while riding on horseback, slapping him with a branch because he sent another workman in his place. But days later, in the moment of her triumph, when she has him in her bedroom, she resists his advances, requiring him to overpower her defenses. Although deeply in love with him and desiring him intensely, she likes to think of their first act of lovemaking as "rape."

Roark is hired by Roger Enright, a businessman, to build a revolutionary kind of apartment house in New York City. Roark designs a spectacularly original and beautiful high-rise building featuring a series of uniquely individualized units, each different from the others, but all adding together to a unified whole. A local newspaper photographer snaps a picture of him standing by the parapet of the East River, his head thrown back, staring up at his building in joyous pride. The towering building overlooking the river attracts significant attention. Consequently, he is hired for other commissions.

Ellsworth Toohey, architecture critic for Gail Wynand's *New York Banner*, a popular newspaper, tries to wreck Roark's career. Toohey, a Marxist intellectual, seeks to establish a Communist dictatorship in America (of the kind in Soviet Russia from which Ayn Rand fled). He knows that Roark is so independent that he will never obey the rule of Communism. If he becomes famous, he will rile many people against the suppressive regime that Toohey seeks to establish.

Dominique joins forces with Toohey. She, too, attempts to wreck Roark's career, but for opposite reasons. Toohey wants to save his collectivist world from Roark; Dominique, on the other hand, wishes to save Roark from the world. She believes Roark's designs are so brilliant and advanced that no world exists for them—that society will inevitably destroy him, and that he will end up as a frustrated, alcoholic, miserable wretch like Henry Cameron. She wants to end Roark's career quickly and painlessly—and at the hands of one who understands and loves him. In brief, for Toohey, this is an act of spiritual murder; for Dominique, it is mercy killing. It is fitting, therefore, that she spends her days wooing clients away from Roark and to Keating—and her nights making love to Roark.

As part of his anti-Roark campaign, Toohey concocts a brilliant scam. One of his servile flunkies, Hopton Stoddard, seeks to build a temple. Toohey convinces Stoddard to hire Roark to design it. Toohey knows that Roark's design will be so revolutionary that it will be unlike any religious structure ever erected—meaning that he will be able to criticize it as a sacrilege and paint Roark as an enemy of religion. This is exactly what occurs. At

Toohey's instigation, Stoddard proceeds to sue Roark, win his case, and take Roark's money to pay for the building's renovations. Roark is now branded as a public enemy. Further, Dominique agonizes over the injustice perpetrated on Roark. It is her worst nightmare come true. She loves and admires a great hero—but a vicious society seeks to destroy him. The only way to anesthetize her pain is to kill off her capacity for hero worship. To accomplish this, she must marry the most degraded moral lowlife she can find. She marries Peter Keating.

In a memorable finale to this chapter, Toohey meets Roark inadvertently at the redesigned former temple. Toohey notes that the two are alone, so nobody can overhear their repartee and Roark can speak freely. Toohey asks Roark what he thinks of him. Without a hint of bravado, speaking the simple truth as he always does, Roark responds that he doesn't think of him. Rand makes it clear here that Roark is so focused on building and living creatively that he wastes no time thinking of such irrational, evil power lusters as Toohey.

Toohey and Dominique's anti-Roark alliance fails. Roark is so independent that they cannot stop him. He needs only the political-economic freedom of the capitalist system. Under its protection, he is free to create—and other independent minds are free to recognize the merit of his designs and hire him. They are free to ignore Toohey's propaganda and Dominique's cocktail parties and lobbying for Keating. And they do.

One of those minds belongs to Gail Wynand, a media and real estate mogul. Although Wynand panders terribly to the crowd, filling his newspaper with the sensationalist material it favors, he himself is an expert judge of talent. He falls in love with and eventually marries Dominique, who, like Toohey, works for his newspaper. Wanting a private country home for himself and his wife, he hires Roark to build it. He also hires Roark for other real estate projects of his, and so Roark's business grows.

Wynand grew up on the West Side of Manhattan, in the harsh slums of Hell's Kitchen. In his youth, he was a brilliant and tough gang leader. In the jobs he held, he typically had innovative ideas to improve the businesses for which he worked. But when he told his lackadaisical bosses, they ignorantly responded, "Shut up, kid, you don't run things around here." Wynand grew up believing that the only way the intelligent and competent men could get positive things accomplished was by ruling the ignorant, irrational dolts who, he believed, constituted the bulk of humanity. Hence, he panders to the most vulgar tastes of the herd while leaving his own brilliant mind and noble values out of the lurid, yellow-press scandal sheet that he publishes. He thus acquires great wealth and political power—but, in so doing, he sells his soul. His own high-minded preferences are demonstrated only in his personal, never in his professional life. He loves Roark's buildings, Roark himself, the idealistic hero worshipper, Dominique, and the beautiful art works sequestered in his private gallery. Dominique marries him to become "Mrs. Wynand Papers," wife of society's most vulgar panderer. Peter Keating was not sufficiently despicable to kill off the nobility of her soul. On her initial view, perhaps Wynand is.

Toohey's flunkies control the commission for a government housing project that poses serious structural problems. Peter Keating covets the commission, but he knows he cannot design it, so he goes to Roark. Roark agrees to do it, and lets Keating get all the credit and money—but on one condition: the building is erected exactly as he designs it. Keating agrees and they sign a contract.

When Roark goes away on vacation with Wynand, Keating is powerless to prevent Toohey and his flunkies from changing Roark's design. When Roark returns, he dynamites the building and turns himself in to stand trial. There is an uproar against the dynamiter of the public housing project. For the first time in his journalistic career, Gail Wynand goes against public opinion. He defends Roark in *The Banner*. His sales drop. When

Toohey attacks Roark in Wynand's paper, Wynand fires him. The union, controlled by Toohey, goes on strike. Wynand and Dominique succeed in putting the paper out by themselves, but nobody buys it. Eventually, Wynand gives in: to save his paper, he denounces Roark and takes Toohey back.

At his trial, Roark defends the right of an individual to his own life, his own mind, and his own work. He is acquitted. Dominique leaves Wynand and marries Roark, the man she truly loves. At the trial, Keating is publicly exposed as a fraud who consciously took credit for another man's work. His career is finished. Roger Enright buys the rights to the housing project from the government and hires

Roark to build it exactly as designed. Gail Wynand shuts down his newspaper, rather than have it controlled by Ellsworth Toohey. Through twelve years of ceaseless scheming, Toohey had sought to seize editorial control of Wynand's newspaper. Wynand destroys all of it in one stroke. Toohey is thereby utterly crushed in both of his attempted power grabs: he can neither stop Roark nor control Wynand's paper. Wynand goes on to hire Roark to build the Wynand Building, the world's tallest skyscraper. Roark thereby reaches significant commercial success—and does so on his own terms.

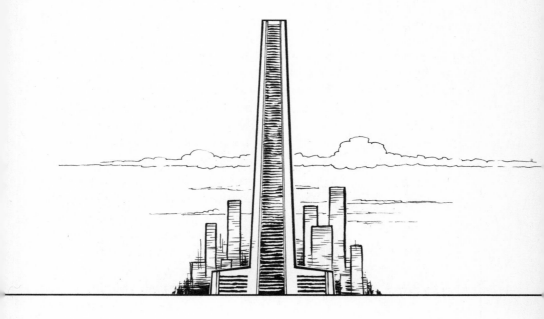

The Main Characters of *The Fountainhead*

Howard Roark is the hero and main character of the story. He is more than a young genius in the field of architecture. He embodies the great men of history who developed new ideas, methods, and inventions, yet were rejected by the very societies that would, in time, most benefit from their work—and who stood up for the truth of their ideas despite persecution. In this way, Roark is like many independent thinkers throughout history—like Socrates, Galileo, Darwin, and others.

Dominique Francon is an independent thinker, who recognizes Roark's genius despite society's rejection of his revolutionary designs; who recognizes Keating's mediocrity, despite society's admiration of his commercial success; and who understands Toohey's evil, despite society's worship of him as a sort of moral saint. But she is tormented by a negative view of human society. She thinks that great men such as Roark have no chance—that they will inevitably be rejected, even destroyed, by society. However, over the course of the story, she witnesses Roark's rise to success, Toohey's failure to stop him, Keating's collapse because of his dishonest methods, and Wynand's defeat because of his pandering to the crowd. Changing her mind, she comes to adopt Roark's belief that it is only the independent, honest men who can truly succeed in this world.

Gail Wynand is a mixed case. He is thoroughly independent in his private life. He loves human beings at their highest and best—that is, for their great achievements and strength of character. He loves Dominique, Roark's buildings, and Roark himself. Nobody tells him who or what belongs in his personal life or in his private art gallery. But in his career, he panders to the lowest tastes of the crowd. None of his own beliefs appear in his newspaper—noth-  ing, for example, about medical breakthroughs, great novels and symphonies, or scientific advances. Rather, his newspaper is filled with lurid crimes and sex scandals. Wynand, so independent in his private life, is completely dependent on the tastes of others— and on their lowest, most vulgar tastes—in his professional life. Eventually, this inner conflict brings him down. He is morally and psychologically broken by the realization that he not only sold his soul—but did so for no gain. Real success, like Roark's, could have come only by devoting his professional life to his own judgment and values, never by betraying them to the most vulgar tastes of the public. Using, in effect, the last gasp of his creative life force, Wynand hires Roark to build the Wynand Building. In a heartbreaking finale, he tells Roark to put into the spirit that is Roark's and that should have been Wynand's.

Peter Keating is a conformist of the worst kind. He is com- pletely dependent on other people for his ideas and be- liefs, his career choice, and his success. For example, he complies with his mother's wish that he become an architect, although he loves painting. He flatters his teachers, professors, and employer, always giving them what they want, and never expressing a thought of his own. He relies on Roark to design his buildings for him while taking all the credit. He marries Dominique Francon, not Catherine Halsey (the woman he loves), because Dominique's beauty, grace, and elegance will impress other people. Ellsworth Toohey is the least independent character in the universe of this book. Keating is second only to him regarding abject dependency on others.

Ellsworth Toohey is a power seeker in every possible way. In his personal life, he is like a cult leader; he takes control of people's lives, takes over their souls, and molds them into his unquestioning followers. In his public life, he is a Marxist intellectual, seeking to establish a Communist dictatorship in America, envisioning himself as an intellectual adviser behind the throne. He tries

to end Roark's career because Roark represents a threat to his authority in the field of architecture. He tries to take control of Wynand's newspaper in order to dictate its editorial policy, enabling him to preach his Communist gospel to millions of readers. He pursues no creative, productive, or independent work. He spends his entire life devising plots, schemes, and scams in order to deceive, manipulate, and control other people. Even Keating can design buildings, however ineptly. But Toohey is not even this creative or independent. All he can do is seek to infiltrate the spirits of others and take them over. Biologically, he is a man; morally, he is a virus—a virus of the soul.

The main point of *The Fountainhead* is the contrast and conflict between independence and dependence—in Ayn Rand's terms, between living a "first-hand" life and a "second-hand" one. An independent person, like Roark, is a thinker—he guides his life and work by means of his own judgment, his own mind. He need not be a genius in the way Roark is—he need only use his own mind to the best of his ability. He must think for himself, arrive at his own conclusions, form his own values, pursue his own interests—and never surrender the things or persons he loves.

But a dependent person, like Keating or Toohey, permits others to dominate his life in some way. He might permit his parents to dictate his career choice, or his family to arrange his marriage, or other authority figures—such as clergy, teachers, or government officials—to fill his unquestioning mind with the specific beliefs they want him to hold. Committing such acts of blind obedience is a form of dependence—and dependence always involves the surrender of a one person's mind to the minds of others. A dependent person permits others to control his life.

In *The Fountainhead*, Ayn Rand argues that a successful, happy life requires independence—whereas dependence leads inevitably to suffering, misery, and even death. On the personal level, only an independent man knows what he wants, forms his own values, and pursues his own loves, refusing to sacrifice them for others. On the social level, only an independent man is willing to stand up for new truths—even when opposed by all of society—and thereby lead to mankind's progress.

A second, related theme involves the relationship between virtue and happiness, honesty and success, morality and practicality. Many people believe that to be successful in this world, a person must be dishonest, corrupt, and deceitful. They say things like, "It's a dog-eat-dog world and I'm gonna get my share," or "It's a jungle out there," or "Either you swim with the sharks or you're eaten by them." They believe that "nice guys finish last," that honest men stand no chance, and that only crooked connivers make it to the top.

Ayn Rand points out the error of this belief. *Roark succeeds only because he's moral.* He forms his own values, knows what he wants, works tirelessly and honestly in pursuit of his goals, and never betrays or relinquishes his dreams—in other words, *he succeeds because of his independence, integrity, and honesty.* Similarly, in real life, the man who uses his own mind to the fullest of its ability, who forms his own convictions and never betrays them, who works as diligently and honestly as possible—this is the individual who rises in the world. He may struggle, but he will not surrender, and, in time, he will succeed.

The Keatings and Tooheys of the world—the manipulators, the power seekers, the dishonest connivers—are not merely eventually exposed and caught; but worse, they have unwittingly surrendered their minds to those people they seek to hoodwink or defraud. They devote their efforts to deceiving others, not to creative or productive work. They exist, therefore, as parasites on the honest efforts of others, and will never reach the levels of success and happiness that they might have reached as honest men.

Chapter 3
Atlas Shrugged

Ayn Rand said that she wrote her greatest novel, *Atlas Shrugged*, to provide a moral defense of capitalism. Prior to *Atlas Shrugged*, defenses of capitalism had been made almost exclusively on economic—not moral—grounds. Its supporters pointed out that capitalism produced more wealth than did any form of socialism, and that the levels of general prosperity achieved under capitalism were always higher.

But, morally, capitalism was always sort of the "red-headed stepchild" of the conservative movement. It featured private ownership of property and a profit motive, qualities encouraging individuals to act in their own self-interest. "But this is selfish!" clamored most moralists. "This is nothing but a 'me, me, me' attitude," said critics from both the socialist left and the religious right. These critics rejected the *egoist* ethics embodied in capitalism, its emphatic support of individuals acting in their own self-interest and pursuing their own success and happiness.

Ayn Rand was among the first to recognize that, in order to fully embrace capitalism, one must first embrace an ethics of "selfishness" properly understood—that is, a moral code of self-interest or egoism. This means that human beings must reject the morality of self-sacrifice that for centuries has taught us that moral goodness lies in providing selfless service to God, to other people, or both.

For human beings to live in freedom, prosperity, and peace, they must finally come to realize that life belongs to the individual, that one is not a servant or slave of others, and that the honest pursuit of one's own happiness—not the providing of selfless service to others—is the hallmark of a moral life. In *Atlas Shrugged*, Ayn Rand clearly presents these moral and philosophical theories in a ringing, riveting tale that its readers find unforgettable.

This book is first and foremost a mystery story, a tale of a man who vows to stop "the motor of the world"—and then does. "The motor of the world?" a reader might ask. "What the hell is that?" Good question, and one to be answered presently. But the story's premise raises other questions as well. Is this person a destroyer or a savior? Is he a villain or a hero? Throughout most of the story, nobody knows for certain.

Dagny Taggart, operating vice-president of Taggart Transcontinental Railroad, considers him a destroyer, a monster. She reviles this unknown shadowy figure as "the evilest man in the world," and threatens to shoot him on sight. But who is he? Is he even real? Nobody knows, but Dagny vows to find out. He poses a terrible threat to that which is most important to her—her railroad and the future of the American economy.

The freight revenue of Taggart Transcontinental, like the profits of every business in this America of the near future, is falling. The country is being pushed toward dictatorship by socialist politicians and the intellectuals—the professors, teachers, journalists, writers, and artists—backing them. Inevitably, as the government takes over ever-increasing portions of the economy, levels of production and prosperity sink lower and lower. The once-mighty and wealthy United States of America slips toward communism—and toward the dictatorship, economic stagnation, and widespread poverty that come with it.

But there is another, even more ominous reason for America's downward spiral. The greatest minds of the country—its leading scientists, inventors, writers, philosophers, artists, and businessmen—are mysteriously retiring and disappearing. Nobody knows where they have gone, or why. Imagine this in real life. Where have all the great minds of the world gone? How and why are they vanishing like that? There would be widespread puzzlement—perhaps even panic. This is the state of the country as presented in *Atlas Shrugged*.

In despair and desperation, the American people often ask a question for which there seems to be no answer: "Who is John Galt?" It essentially means, "What's the use?" The country is collapsing and all is lost. The question conveys a mentality of doom and gloom—an end-of-the-world sense of despair that an optimistic, "never-say-die" kind of person like Dagny hates. Nobody seems to know who is John Galt—from where the question came—or even if such a person literally exists or not. The puzzling, unanswerable question is part of the mystery that permeates the universe of this story.

Dagny struggles to rebuild the Rio Norte Line, linking the industrialized state of Colorado to the rest of the nation. But instead of constructing it from steel, she chooses to use Rearden Metal, a new alloy invented by steel manufacturer Hank Rearden. Since the new metal is untried, her choice causes a public outcry.

For example, the government-funded and -run State Science Institute (SSI) burns with envy. After all, if a private, profit-driven individual like Hank Rearden creates such a life-promoting technology, then what justifies coercing the taxpayers to fund the SSI? What justifies an end to private research and the coercion of great minds to work exclusively for the government? In the absence of facts, evidence, or hard data, the SSI releases a craftily worded statement to the press, claiming it is possible that, under certain unspecified stresses, some unpredictable problem with the metal might potentially appear. It is a vague, non-objective, unscientific smear, but it is backed by the prestigious State Science Institute—and it causes a furor among the press and the general public.

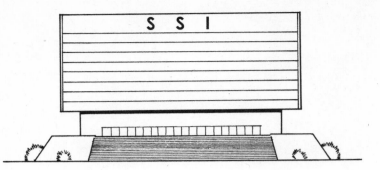

Nevertheless, Dagny and Rearden push ahead against great obstacles—for she is an engineer and he a metallurgist, and they recognize the greatness of the metal. Telling the SSI and its horde of admiring media flunkies to go to hell, they keep working against enormous opposition, complete the rail line, and then run the first train on it with overwhelming success.

WHAT POWER ON EARTH WILL ENABLE A BRIDGE OF LIGHT-WEIGHT REARDEN METAL TO STAND UP UNDER THE STRESSES OF A MULTI-TON FREIGHT TRAIN?

MY JUDGEMENT.

Dagny and Rearden become lovers. Rearden believes that sex is based on low, animalistic urges, and is therefore tortured by his intense desire for this woman he admires so much. By contrast, Dagny believes that sex is a proper celebration of one's own worth and one's chosen lover, and therefore takes joyous pride in her intimate sexual acts with this man she so greatly loves and admires.

On vacation, they discover the remnants of a new kind of motor left moldering on a scrap pile in an abandoned factory. The invention would have revolutionized industry and human life—much as the introduction of steel, automobiles, and electric power did. How could someone have abandoned it like that? Dagny and Rearden can find no answer, so Dagny launches a search to locate the inventor—but it runs into a dead end. She then hires a promising young scientist to attempt the motor's reconstruction.

But the socialist rulers keep expanding their power over the lives of individual Americans. Desperate to prop up their failing policies, they pass legislation forbidding workers to retire, change jobs, or relocate to new areas—thereby chaining American citizens to their current occupations, effectively enslaving them. In defiance of the socialist regime and its suppressive laws, many workers quit or move away. Dagny, terrified that her individualistic young scientist will rebel and disappear, flies to Utah, where he works, to convince him to stay on. She is too late. The destroyer, whoever he is, has gotten to him first. The destroyer's plane takes the scientist away just as Dagny arrives.

She chases after them, but crash-lands in the Colorado Rockies. Here, in a valley, she finds all of the great thinkers who so mysteriously retired and disappeared. Here are the scientists, the inventors, the business leaders, the writers, the artists, and the philosophers that the country so desperately needs. She discovers that they are on strike—against the socialist dictatorship that decrees that men's lives belong to the state. And they are on strike against the moral code underlying that form of government—the belief that moral goodness lies not in a man's pursuit of his own happiness, but in sacrificing himself for others. They will not return until the pack of sniveling moochers in Washington, DC, learn to respect and protect their right to their own lives, their own brains, and their own profit.

Dagny finds that there is a "John Galt"—and that he is both the inventor of the motor and the destroyer who has drained the country of its brains. He is also the one who initiated the strike. During her time in the valley, Dagny and Galt fall in love. But Galt refuses to act on his feelings so long as Dagny remains a "scab"—a person who continues to work in the outer world, lending her mind and great talents to the system established by the socialist dictators, and thereby helping to prop up their evil regime. Dagny, who originally vowed to shoot the destroyer on sight, now wants to rip his clothes off and make passionate love to him!

Despite her love for Galt and her sympathy for the ideas held by the strikers, Dagny refuses to give up her railroad and join the strike. However, when she returns to the outer world, she finds the system of the "looters" in a dire state of collapse. The president, known as "Mr. Thompson," sets out to make a radio address to the country, trying to calm its fears. But John Galt, using the power of his revolutionary motor, preempts the president's address—Mr. Thompson's sorry time is up—with his own.

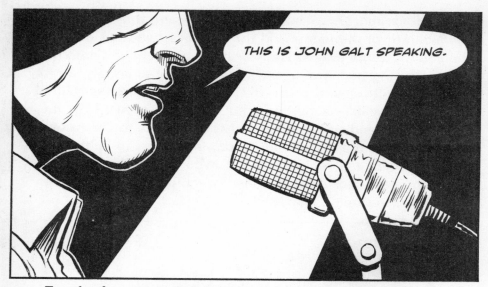

For the first time, Galt publicly announces the existence of the strike, the reasons for it, and the conditions of the strikers' return. Given the almost complete collapse of American society, millions of people can now understand Galt's words and his reasons. His speech sparks a light bulb effect for many of the American people: "Ah hah! Now I get it!" they respond. "Now I know why the great minds have vanished, and which principles and policies are necessary to bring them back." This is neither a quote nor a paraphrase—just a point of explanation I made up.

The government—in its
own brutal, power-lusting
fashion—understands Galt
all too well. Its agents track
Galt down and take him
prisoner. They want to use
his genius to solve the
country's economic crisis
and save their socialist
policies. When Galt refuses
to cooperate, the dictators
torture him in an attempt
to make him become the
economic dictator of the

nation. Seeing that they will kill Galt rather than release him,
Dagny joins the strike. She and Galt's striking allies rescue him.
With no remorse, she guns down one of the soldiers guarding
the torture chamber, and they escape with Galt back to the valley. In time, the dictators' regime collapses. The strikers are then
free to return to and rebuild the outer world.

The Main Characters of *Atlas Shrugged*

John Galt, the inventor of the motor and the originator of the strike, is an extraordinary genius. As a philosopher, physicist, and statesman, he advances—indeed revolutionizes—human understanding. At the core of his genius is his rational mind. Galt is a *rational thinker*, a man willing to acknowledge all facts regardless of his feelings about them, even when those facts are frightening, painful, or unpleasant. Galt's strike is, in large part, on behalf of his conviction that rational thought—not faith or feelings—is responsible for human well-being. For example, it is with the mind that one learns how to grow food, design and build homes, and cure diseases, among countless other skills. Further, Galt argues, the mind must be free and protected—never suppressed—by a proper government. Each individual has the right to his own thinking—to employ his mind in support of his own life and happiness. Galt lives by and fights for these ideas.

Because of the strike, Galt must abandon his revolutionary motor and any hope of wooing Dagny. These are agonizing truths to face. But despite the pain of such losses, Galt does not see them as sacrifices. He realizes that, given the state of the world, he has no chance for the success and happiness he desires. His only chance lies in changing the world to make possible the success of honest and rational men. Galt tells Dagny that it is not that he doesn't suffer—but that he knows the unimportance of such suffering in the face of what must be accomplished.

Galt is the story's main character, even though he operates behind the scenes for the first two-thirds of the novel. But **Dagny Taggart** is its primary narrator, and most of the story's action is seen through her eyes. She agrees with all of Galt's main ideas, which is an important reason that she falls in love with him. For

example, she agrees that the rational mind is mankind's tool of survival—and that the mind must be free to think, create, progress, and express itself in any form it will. Each individual has the right to his own life, his own mind, and the pursuit of his own happiness. To all of these ideas, Dagny is as passionately committed as is Galt. But she loves her railroad too much to abandon it. She believes the "looters"— the thieving politicians and the intellectuals who back them—are simply honestly mistaken, not evil, and will eventually see the error of their ways. She believes that she can convince them.

But when Dagny sees that they will murder Galt rather than abandon their policies and their power, she realizes that they are evil and joins the strike. She loves Galt so much—and is so deeply committed to the right of each individual to live in freedom—that this peaceful, productive, constructive woman even shoots and kills a man guarding the dungeon in which the government's flunkies torture John Galt.

Hank Rearden, Dagny's lover, is a brilliant industrialist, the world's greatest producer of steel and the inventor of Rearden Metal. But he makes two critical errors. Influenced by the legacy of religion, he holds that man's mind (or spirit) is noble, capable of high-minded moral principles—but that his body is low and consumed by base desires for gratification, sex, material comforts, and wealth. As a sad consequence, he feels guilty about the wealth he's earned and the passionate, loving relationship he has with Dagny, rather than proud and joyous.

Rearden agrees with Dagny and the strikers that an individual must live for his own happiness; like them, he is an egoist. But he also believes that he cannot judge the moral beliefs of others. For example, his family members mooch off of him shamelessly, and the politicians loot the wealth he has created. Rearden is horrified by their actions, but, like Dagny, believes they are honestly mistaken. He refuses to judge them and believes he can show them that they are wrong. As  events unfold, he comes to realize that the moochers and looters are not merely wrong—they are evil—and he joins the strike. He comes to the realization that he can and must judge as evil those surviving by sucking his blood. He guiltlessly and joyously throws them off his back—Atlas shrugs—and will live fully for his own happiness.

Francisco d'Anconia is one of the world's wealthiest men, a copper producer, and a great mind. He is a childhood friend of Dagny's, and as teenagers they were each other's first loves. Francisco still loves her, but, because she is a "scab," he has to give her up for the strike. Francisco met Galt in college and they are close friends. He is the first one to join Galt's strike. Francisco has the difficult job of gradually

liquidating d'Anconia Copper to prevent its wealth from being looted by the socialist governments of the world. He postures as a dissolute playboy, appearing to squander vast amounts of his wealth. But in reality he is a primary recruiting agent for the strike, and the man most responsible for showing Hank Rearden the errors he has made, enabling Rearden to experience the joyous liberation that he so abundantly deserves. In the end, although he loses Dagny to Galt, Francisco is triumphant: the strike succeeds, the strikers return to the world, and he is free to be the productive giant that he is.

James Taggart, Dagny's brother, is one of the arch-villains of the story. He is the president of Taggart Transcontinental, and a confirmed altruist—one who believes that an individual is morally obligated to others. As such, he is a prominent member of the socialist regime that forcibly prevents individuals from pursuing their own happiness and coerces them to serve their "less fortunate" brothers and sisters. Taggart, like Ellsworth Toohey in *The Fountainhead*, and like many Fascists and Communists in real life, is a relentless power seeker, as a consistent altruist must be. For if moral goodness lies in sacrificing oneself for others, and most free people will reject that for the pursuit of their own happiness, what can an altruist do about such "immorality"? The logical answer is to establish a socialist state that will force such "selfish" individuals to perform their moral obligations to others. This is exactly what Taggart and his cronies do. America, under the rule of Taggart and his cohorts, becomes a socialist state.

Robert Stadler is another of the story's major villains. He is a brilliant scientist, but he believes that people are generally stupid and uninterested in serious issues. They would never voluntarily support science and research. Therefore, they must be forced to do so. He convinces the government to establish a State Science Institute, which is funded by money confiscated from honest men by government taxes. Stadler is a classic "egghead" who deals only with theoretical issues and broad abstractions, rather than with practical matters and everyday life. For example, when Dagny shows him the remnants of Galt's motor and manuscript, he is impressed by the problems of theoretical physics that the inventor solved, but contemptuous that Galt used his great brainpower to create something as practical as a motor. He disdains it as though it were of no more importance than a piece of plumbing or an electric can opener. Although brilliant, Stadler is a pompous ass who seeks power over the masses of people he deems to be his inferiors. In an attempt to seize control of a government installation of weapons of mass destruction and establish himself as a sort of feudal lord over the area, he reaches a justly deserved death.

THE *RATIONAL MIND* IS THE MOST IMPORTANT PART OF HUMAN BEINGS AND HUMAN LIFE.

Ayn Rand's characters were often criticized. Some critics complained that her heroes were "larger than life" and totally unrealistic. Some claimed that her characters were underdeveloped and merely mouthpieces for theories and ideas. However, Ayn Rand herself believed that human beings are capable of great achievements and heroism, and that, in fact, the history of mankind shows many towering heroes. She believed that the rational mind is the most important resource of human life—that people (and society more broadly) are motivated by the ideas they hold—and that her fictional characters properly understood and expressed those ideas. She and her critics held sharply different ideas about human nature in both life and literature.

Ayn Rand presents two main ideas in this book. One is that the human mind is responsible for all the good things that human life and happiness depend on. For example, food must be grown and livestock domesticated, which requires knowledge of agricultural science—and therefore reasoning. Medical cures must be researched and developed, requiring knowledge of biology. Houses and buildings must be designed and constructed, requiring knowledge of architecture, engineering, and mathematics. Further, the genius of the mind creates great works of art. And it is the mind—not screaming irrationality or brute force—that is necessary to resolve human disagreements, whether interpersonal or international.

At the root of such values are thinking and knowledge, Rand pointed out, not faith in the supernatural, not following our feelings or urges, not creating in drug-induced, delusional states. Hard manual labor is certainly an important part of growing and harvesting food, building houses and automobiles, and accomplishing many other necessary tasks, but first the knowledge of how to grow, build, and create these things must be gained. Primitive man certainly did not lack muscle power—rather, he lacked knowledge.

The second major point of the book is that the creative human mind requires political-economic freedom in order, for example, to write novels, compose symphonies, devise scientific or philosophical theories, and make technological advances. Under a capitalist system in which each individual holds an inalienable right to his own life, his own mind, and the pursuit of his own happiness, he is free to think and express his thinking, start his own business, invent new devices, manufacture new products, or create works of art. It is the freedom of the capitalist system that, by liberating the most progressive thinkers in society, is responsible for the enormous creation of material and cultural wealth in society.

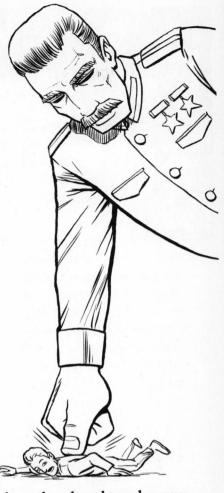

On the other hand, under any dictatorship—whether tribal, religious, military, Fascist, Communist, or any other kind—the freethinking human mind is stifled, forced to bow to authority. Those who do not obey are imprisoned, exiled, enslaved, tortured, or murdered. Therefore, political-economic freedom is not a human luxury, but a requirement of human survival and well-being.

Ayn Rand's critics have savaged this book. Their criticisms have ranged across a broad field of objections. Some have claimed the book is too long and its plot too complicated, convoluted, or ponderous. Some have argued that its characters are cardboard figures, not fully developed flesh-and-blood human beings. Some have alleged that it is preachy, dogmatic, didactic, or simply non-artistic. Some have even claimed that the atheistic, secular philosophy expressed in this book is akin to Marxism—and that the book therefore advocates Communist totalitarianism.

The ever-growing number of Ayn Rand's supporters counter that *Atlas Shrugged* presents a brilliantly plotted story that has drawn millions of breathless readers, who often can't put it down until they complete it, despite its 1,000-page length. Dagny Taggart, many say, is one of the great heroines of world literature—and characters such as Hank Rearden and Francisco d'Anconia are unforgettable. The novel is deeply philosophical, but the philosophy is not merely discussed: *it is dramatized brilliantly in every action, event, and scene.* Further, the philosophy presented in the action glorifies the mind, individual rights, and political-economic freedom—and stands in direct opposition to the materialism, collectivism, and dictatorship of the Communists.

Such controversy over *Atlas Shrugged*, even after half a century, has only just begun. It promises to rage for centuries—as evident, for example, by the split between intellectuals and the American people on this issue. At the turn of the new millennium, lists were compiled of the hundred most important books of the twentieth century. One such list was compiled by the Modern Library division of Random House. The in-house panel of experts did not mention *Atlas Shrugged*. However, readers around the world, voting on-line in an Internet poll, selected *Atlas Shrugged* as number one.

With the publication of this book, Ayn Rand became a national celebrity, both vilified and lionized. Professional educators and intellectuals, for the most part, either ignored the book or sharply criticized it—but millions of readers love both the story and its philosophy.

It was in *Atlas Shrugged* that Ayn Rand presented her radical philosophy of Objectivism—and it was this book that created an Objectivist movement.

Chapter 4
The Creation of Ayn Rand's Philosophy

Ayn Rand named her philosophy "Objectivism" for reasons that we will soon see. But why bother with philosophy at all? Most people consider the subject a boring waste of time—just a lot of hot air blown around by a bunch of tiresome windbags. And anyway, isn't it impossible to come up with any right answers to the questions? Philosophy is not like math or science, right? If there are no wrong answers, then one blowhard's opinion is just as good as another's. Who wants to waste time on a useless subject like that?

But Ayn Rand strongly disagreed with such a negative assessment of philosophy. Indeed, she wrote an essay called "Philosophy—Who Needs It." Her answer was: all of us. Every human being, and every society, needs it. In fact, philosophy is so much a part of human life that none of us can escape holding a philosophy! Every last one of us holds a philosophy—whether we realize it or not, whether we want to or not.

How can that be? How can everyone, including violent criminals and gangsters, hold a philosophy of life? What about drunks and drug addicts? And morons and illiterates? Was Ayn Rand crazy? What did she mean?

To start, philosophy deals with the most basic questions of human life. The whole field can be reduced to attempts to answer three basic questions: First, what kind of world do we live in? Second, how do we gain knowledge of such a world? And third, how should we live our lives, i.e., what is good? These three questions are so important—and so fundamental—that no adult human being could survive for even a short period of time without some kind of answer to all of them.

For example, take the prominence of religion in many societies. *Religion is a type of philosophy.* It attempts to give answers to every philosophical question. Irrational, inadequate, and harmful answers, in Ayn Rand's judgment, but answers nevertheless. What are they? For starters, religion claims that the world was created by God and is run by God. He created the laws of nature; He governs them; and He has a plan for the world. Whatever happens in His world, for good or for ill, happens in accordance with His plan.

Questions and answers about the nature of the universe—whether religious or secular, otherworldly or worldly—are addressed in a branch of philosophy known as *metaphysics.* Religion provides one type of answer to these questions, but hardly the only type. From the standpoint of a religious type of philosophy, we might ask: If this is the nature of the world, how do human beings gain knowledge of it? We cannot observe God with our eyes, ears, or sense of touch—not like we can sense physical objects. So how do we know about Him? How do we know He exists, that He created and governs the world, and that He causes various miracles? The only way we can gain such "knowledge" is by means of faith.

We start with a "revealed text," such as the Bible or the Koran, a book supposedly written by men who were divinely inspired, and accept its teachings without question. So, for example, if the Bible says that burning bushes speak, men live inside whales, women are turned to pillars of salt, or virgins give birth, then these beliefs, no matter how bizarre, must be accepted by a religious man who is faithful to the teachings of the Bible. On the basis of faith, any claim, no matter how absurd, must be blindly accepted.

HEY WHAT'S UP?

VACANCY

If we accept such claims as a matter of faith, then what should we do with them? How should we live? What is good—and what is evil? Following the most basic philosophy of religion, only one course of action could possibly be good: to obey God. Moral goodness lies in acceptance of and obedience to God's commandments. Evil is disregarding or disobeying those commandments. If God is the all-powerful creator and governor of the universe, then no other way of living could possibly be virtuous.

Some might argue that religion is a simple-minded, poor man's approach to philosophy—but a type of philosophy it nevertheless remains. It seeks to answer all three of philosophy's basic questions. What kind of world do we inhabit? One created and governed by an all-powerful spirit of the universe. How do we learn the important truths of such a world? By means of faith in the Bible and in the clergy. What should we do? We must obey God's commandments.

But how do we make sense of the claim that all human beings necessarily hold a philosophy of life, even violent criminals and gangsters? A criminal survives by victimizing innocent people—by robbing, beating, even murdering them. He does not seek survival by means of productive work. For example, he does not grow

food, build houses, drive a bus or a cab, or perform any other useful work. He does not produce any of the goods or services upon which human life depends. He does not deal directly with nature, cultivate produce from the land, build structures to house families or businesses, or create wealth in any other way. His attitude is: let other people do all of that hard work—and I'll rob them.

LET OTHER PEOPLE DO ALL OF THE HARD WORK—AND I'LL *ROB* THEM.

What type of world does he live in? To him, it's one that is entirely social. Other people are his sole reality. To him, nature— its rules, its life-generating requirements, its inflexible and unchanging laws—are irrelevant and not to be considered. All that matters is that other people can be tricked, forced, or bullied into providing what he wants. Is there a God who prohibits such criminal actions? Who cares? Are there laws of nature that require human beings to work productively in support of their lives? Who knows and who cares, if I can get what I want from exploiting human society?

How does a criminal gain knowledge in such a world? Notice that a criminal acts on the crudest of human impulses—the desire for unearned wealth, material possessions, bodily gratification. He is guided by his urges and feelings. He doesn't seek knowledge by reading the Bible and accepting its teachings on faith. He does not study science, mathematics, or philosophy— or by any other applied use of his mind. The only "thinking" he does is to concoct scams or schemes to gratify his urges without getting caught. But it is his urges that set the fundamental terms of his life; they are always the primary consideration. He accepts his feelings and desires as unquestioned and absolute. If he feels something, then it is true for him; it is right for him.

What, then, does the criminal believe is the right thing to do? To follow his feelings, act on his impulses, and satisfy his urges. How does he treat or relate to other human beings? According to his code of conduct, they are there to be used for his gratification— and, if necessary, to be exploited and victimized.

All human beings, even the brutes among mankind, require some type of philosophy by which to guide their lives. In her work, Ayn Rand stresses repeatedly that philosophy is an inescapable necessity of human life. The only choices we have are whether to think consciously about and understand our philosophy, or simply to hold our view of the world at the level of feelings. Do we form our basic ideas independently, or do we unquestioningly accept the ideas held by our families or society? We can refuse to think about the philosophical ideas we accept—but then we are at the mercy of the ideas held by other people. We are never able to escape the need of philosophy.

KNOCK KNOCK...

Objectivism and You: Perfect Together

Ayn Rand was a great salesman for philosophy as a fundamental necessity of every human life. But the specific theories she held differed widely from the ideas generally dominant among philosophers in the modern world. For example, there is a reason that she named her philosophy "Objectivism." She believed that truth and values are *objective*. In other words, knowledge of philosophy, science, morality, and every other subject is based in fact—not in the opinions, beliefs, or feelings of any individual or group.

Why is this controversial?—many people might ask. Who doesn't believe this? Isn't such a claim simply common sense? Well, this might be the dominant view in the field of science, but the prevailing approaches to morality and philosophy are far different. Almost all modern philosophers (and many intelligent laymen) believe that truth is "socially constructed." Put simply, they believe that an individual is raised in a society, educated in that society, and his beliefs are shaped—or "conditioned"—by that society. In their view, facts have little or nothing to do with it. An individual's thinking, beliefs, and ideas are simply absorbed from the dominant beliefs of his society.

TRUTH AND VALUES ARE *OBJECTIVE*.

For example, Western society highly values reason, science, technology, individual rights, political-economic freedom, and capitalism. But these are just the preferences of many people in the Western world, according to most modern philosophers. Differing beliefs dominate in other parts of the world, including fundamentalist religion, mysticism, tribalism, and every variant of socialism, statism, and dictatorship. Modern thinkers hold that all these varying theories simply represent social differences of opinions—no theory is truer or better than any other— and no individual raised and educated under one set of ideas can judge (or even understand) the dominant ideas of foreign nations or societies.

To Ayn Rand, this is nonsense. For example, it is a fact that many diseases are caused by germs, no matter how many societies believe that they are caused by evil spirits or God's punishment of sinful man, or any similarly mistaken beliefs. In another example, there is no evidence whatever to support the claim that a person's moral character is based on his racial makeup—and that millions of people in Nazi Germany believed such vicious nonsense did nothing to change that basic fact. Indeed, human society once believed the planet Earth to be flat—when, in fact, it has always been round. Truth is based on the facts of reality, regardless of what beliefs are held by human society.

This assertion is a major theme in *The Fountainhead*. In that novel, Ayn Rand tells the story of an innovative thinker who throws off the architectural beliefs of his society and introduces new ones of his own. Throughout history, the author pointed out, the greatest heroes of mankind have been original thinkers who rejected the core beliefs of their societies, formed new ideas, and struggled for years against social norms to have the new theories accepted. Socrates, Copernicus, Galileo, Darwin, and Pasteur are all examples of this phenomenon. It can certainly be argued that Ayn Rand herself is an example.

An individual—a *thinking individual*—is not a helpless pawn of his society, its educational system, and its core beliefs. He is able to look at the realities of the world, at nature, at facts, and think independently. This is how many individuals come to reject the beliefs of their families, their clergy, their teachers, their professors, their governments, and their societies in general. This is how independent freethinkers have arisen, battled against the entrenched conservative beliefs of their societies, and ultimately established the truth of their new theories.

According to Ayn Rand, ethics and morality are no different from other intellectual disciplines; they, too, are based on objective facts. For example, many societies throughout history (and continuing to this day) have tragically believed in the moral rightness of human slavery. But, in fact, an individual human being has an inalienable right to his own life—and slavery is hideously wrong. For example, some Communists have believed it morally proper to murder millions of middle class (or "bourgeois") individuals, and the Nazis have similarly believed it morally proper to butcher millions of "racially inferior" peoples. But regardless of such widespread beliefs in those societies, the fact remains that murder is morally wrong.

Ethics and philosophy, as well as science, are grounded in facts—not in the beliefs of society. In these cases, the primary facts are those of human nature, and what is necessary for human beings to do in order to flourish in their lives on earth. That Ayn Rand upholds the objectivity of truth and moral values in her work is the main reason that her ideas are rejected by modern intellectuals. But it is not the only reason, as we will see.

Rand's theories have much more in common with the great ancient philosophers, notably Aristotle, than with the moderns. Generally, according to the Greeks, knowledge was gained by looking to nature, not to society—and the good was based in the facts of human nature, not in the beliefs of the many. Therefore, Rand may well have been less controversial in the ancient world than in the modern world.

In brief, her philosophy of Objectivism claims that facts do not depend on the beliefs of any individual, group, society, or even God, if such a being exists. Truth must be based on facts, not beliefs. Therefore, reason—not feelings or faith—is the means by which human beings gain knowledge. The reasoning mind is the means by which mankind creates every good or service that its survival and prosperity depend on. When a human individual acts in accordance with his rational nature, he has the ability to achieve at a very high level—and even to be a hero. The good is to be rational, and to reject all forms of irrationality. In fact, in order to live, an individual must pursue his own loves, his own values, and his own happiness. Sacrificing the self is morally wrong. Therefore, every individual has an inalienable right to his own life, his own mind, and the pursuit of his own happiness. A proper government recognizes, upholds, and protects this principle of individual rights. The proper political-economic system is, therefore, laissez-faire capitalism.

Ayn Rand's thinking is original and revolutionary. It generally goes against most of the main ideas held by today's professors, teachers, writers, critics, and intellectuals. Therefore, in her own lifetime and continuing to this day, she is generally rejected by intellectuals. For example: whereas Rand endorsed the principle of individual rights, most modern thinkers maintain that society, in various forms, takes precedence over the individual— and that an individual must, properly, be subordinated to its needs. But the primary reason of Rand's rejection is her uncompromising commitment to independence and objectivity: whereas she upholds the ability (and need) of a thinking individual to formulate principles and values based on facts—and to critically examine, at times even to reject the beliefs of his society—modern thinkers generally maintain that an individual's core beliefs are absorbed automatically and involuntarily from the society in which he is raised. Regarding both knowledge and moral responsibilities, the moderns generally uphold the dominance of society over the individual—while Rand upholds the opposite.

REASON - NOT FEELINGS OR FAITH - IS THE MEANS BY WHICH HUMAN BEINGS GAIN KNOWLEDGE.

Chapter 5
The Philosophy of Objectivism

People often poke fun at philosophers by depicting them as having their heads in the clouds, asking such questions as "What is the meaning of life?" Although philosophers sometimes deserve to be ridiculed, this is nevertheless a serious question—and a good one. What is life all about, anyway? Is it about obeying God, attaining salvation in a higher world, serving one's community or nation, gratifying one's bodily desires—or what?

IT'S PRETTY WILD UP HERE...

Ayn Rand had her own distinctive answer to this question. According to her theory, values are the meaning of life. The things and persons that an individual loves and cherishes—these are what provide meaning in his life. So, like Howard Roark in *The Fountainhead*, a person might love architecture—or, similar to Dagny Taggart in *Atlas Shrugged*, an individual might love engineering and railroading. A person might passionately pursue an education in biology, literature, computer science, or any other subject of particular interest. A person might seek a productive career in business, construction, nursing, or any other field of work. An individual might fervently seek to have children and raise a family. Another individual might intensely desire a passionate, intimate romantic relationship. He might love art, education, earning wealth, or cultivating meaningful friendships—or perhaps all of them at once—or any other good, healthy, rational, life-promoting pursuit in human existence.

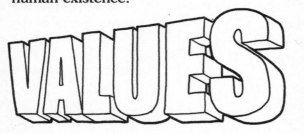

These are all examples of *values*—the things or persons an individual considers so valuable, worthy, and important that they impel him to goal-directed action. In other words, values are the objects of actions. For example, a person who desires an education will work hard in his studies; a young person who wants to play high school basketball will practice for long hours to improve his skills; a father who wants a close relationship with his son or daughter will carve out quality time in his busy schedule to spend with his child. Values, as Ayn Rand puts it, are those things that motivate a person to act in order to obtain or keep them.

If deeply cherished personal values are the meaning of life, then it follows that it is right for an individual to pursue those values, to achieve his goals, to fulfill himself—and never to surrender or betray what is most important to him. This principle is what Ayn Rand called the "virtue of selfishness."

To be "selfish" in her sense of the term is a very, very good thing—and difficult to achieve. It requires an individual's unbroken dedication to the things and persons most important to him or her. Imagine all the different kinds of things a person might want to do, such as start his own software company, open a beauty salon, get a Ph.D., write a novel, compose music, play major league baseball, perform on Broadway, earn a black belt in karate, rear a family of healthy, happy, fulfilled children, or one of countless other goals. In and of themselves, these dreams are difficult to attain—they take a great deal of goal-oriented study, practice, hard work, and devotion. Many people do not want to pay such a price to reach their ends.

Making matters more difficult, such a "selfish" person might have to overcome powerful social obstacles. For example, a teenager who strongly desires to become an actor might have parents who strenuously object and insist that he will go to medical school and become a doctor. Such a young man must have great personal integrity and strength of purpose to resist the family pressures in order to reach those goals that will provide his life meaning and happiness.

Or, in another example, an original thinker forms a new theory or method that he is certain is true, revolutionary, and important. But it is so new and revolutionary that most of society rejects it, considers it dangerous, and vilifies him, treating him as a social outcast or enemy. Like most people, he yearns for social acceptance and finds public rejection painful, but is he willing to surrender his life's work, his understanding of truth, and his own judgment to be accepted? This is a painful choice—and it takes great strength of character to remain committed to one's own vision, ideals, and ultimately the values that give meaning and joy to one's life.

An unyielding commitment to personal values is the essence of Ayn Rand's theory of *egoism*—the moral code that deems it *morally right* for an individual to pursue his own happiness, and morally wrong to sacrifice the self. This theory conflicts with the moral code that has dominated the Western world for more than two thousand years. Both religion and modern socialism claim that morality requires a person to *sacrifice himself* for some higher good. Such a good might lie in selfless service to God, the family, or the state—or all of the above.

Rand's point is that human life itself requires the achievement of values. We survive and prosper only to the extent that we work to gain all of the important things in life—education, a productive career, a strong character, close friends, an intimate relationship, children, and so on. Can we gain happiness if we give up any of these critical values? Can we even survive if we sacrifice our career and the money we earn from it?

Life itself necessitates the attainment of values. Plants must dig their roots into the soil and grow their leaves toward the sun in order to absorb life-sustaining nutrients and sunlight. Similarly, animals must hunt, build nests, burrow holes, migrate to warmer climes, and perform numerous other activities to gain the food, shelter, and warmth that they need to remain alive. Finally, human beings must grow crops, study math, philosophy, and science, build cities, and create governments to gain the food, knowledge, and civilizations that support human life.

To put it simply: a person can live only by gaining these goods. He cannot live by surrendering them. He can live by working hard for his values, or die by sacrificing them. Egoism—the code supporting the attainment of personal values—is the code of life. Altruism—the code supporting the sacrifice of values to God or society—is the code of death.

Does this mean that a person who is selfish in Ayn Rand's sense of the term cannot help others? Not at all. Several important points must be made. First, the best thing you can do for another person is to encourage him to achieve his own values, to show him that it is morally right for him to work hard in pursuit of his own happiness, and to protect his legal right to do so. You should also show him that it is morally wrong to sacrifice the things most important to him for somebody else, which will only lead him to frustration and misery. Moreover, it is morally wrong for anyone—whether family, government, clergy, society in general, or anyone else—to demand his sacrifice. *To care genuinely about a person is to care about him achieving his values and happiness—i.e., to encourage him to be egoistic.*

Second, a rational human being, working honestly in the pursuit of his own happiness, necessarily loves, befriends, and cares about many people—for example, his closest friends, his girlfriend or wife, children, family members, neighbors, colleagues, and others. To help the people he cares about the most will make him happy.

For example, it is often called a "sacrifice" when a loving parent works hard to support his child, and does without a new car or other conveniences to save for his child's education. But, in Ayn Rand's view, this is a properly egoistic action on the parent's part, not an altruistic one—because the parent values the child far more than the conveniences he gives up, which are trivial in comparison. A loving parent might be willing to walk on his knees from New York to Los Angeles and back in order to gain his child's well-being—and consider it a bargain. That's how important the child's health and happiness are to him.

Third, helping others is an individual's choice, not a duty—something to be done if and only if it is a personal value, not because it is an obligation. Genuine benevolence—kindness or goodwill—for our brothers and sisters is a priceless value. How do we teach it? Ayn Rand's answer: by teaching an individual that his life belongs to him; that he should pursue his own happiness; that he has the moral and legal right to do so; and that it is right for him to help others only if and to the extent that he voluntarily wants to. *This ensures that others are not a cause of sacrifice on his part.* They are not a threat to his values, his happiness, or his well-being. He realizes fully that no person has the moral right to demand that he sacrifice those things or persons most dear to him—and that he has no moral right to demand it of others. This realization liberates him from the threat of servitude to others—thus freeing him to understand the great potential value of other men and women, and to form positive relationships with them.

Fourth, if we as human beings genuinely care about our brothers and sisters, and we value love and goodwill, where is the goodwill toward the poor bastard who is called upon to sacrifice? Where, for example, is the kindness toward the son called upon by his family to give up the woman he wants to marry or to sacrifice the career choice he values? There is none. To call upon another to sacrifice his values and happiness is cruel, ruthless, and inhumane.

Fifth, the question arises: Is it in a man's self-interest to be a self-indulgent brute, willing to victimize innocent others to promote his own pleasure, wealth, or power? Ayn Rand's answer is an emphatic "no." At the common-sense level, it is very much in a rational person's self-interest to have positive relations with his fellow man—to have close friends, an intimate romantic relationship, family, etc.—and not engage in the endless, seething conflict that is the inevitable result of abusing innocent others.

Let's take this point a bit deeper: Human beings survive and prosper by means of honest, productive effort, by working as diligently as possible *to create the values* that their lives and happiness depend on. Human beings do not prosper by underhanded, conniving, duplicitous, or criminal means; rather, we survive and prosper by means of honest achievement. We are not sharks or other types of predatory creatures; rather, we are rational, creative, productive beings. It is in this type of life that a human being's self-interest lies—and it is this type of life that Ayn Rand upholds in her work.

Notice the similarity between the code of self-sacrifice and the code of cynical exploitation. *They both support the sacrifice of one human being to another.* The code of self-sacrifice endorses *a man sacrificing himself to others.* The cynical code of victimizing others endorses *a man sacrificing others to himself.* This is the only difference between them. Both are essentially primitive moral codes that have never outgrown the need of human sacrifice. Neither of them upholds the idea that individuals should honestly create the values their lives require—and then interact with each other voluntarily, peacefully, and to mutual benefit.

Last, it is a very simple matter for a rational human being to help himself and others simultaneously. Rational people literally do it every day. In one example, which we've already mentioned, by doing things for a friend, family member, child, lover, or another beloved person, an individual makes both himself and the associate happy. In another example, a teacher or doctor who works hard to be the best at his profession he can be—who, by means of conscientious effort, earns a living, takes pride in his work, and enjoys the reward of seeing his students or patients flourish—benefits both himself and others. In fact, any type of productive work a person does will benefit both himself and his customers, clients, or employers. It is eminently possible—indeed, not at all difficult—to help both oneself and others. *But it is impossible for an individual both to fulfill and to sacrifice himself—this is a contradiction akin to a round square.* Helping both the self and others is not difficult to attain—as long as it is done according to an egoistic code. The code and actions of self-sacrifice must be repudiated. Again, these points are what Ayn Rand meant by the "virtue of selfishness."

The Virtue of Selfishness

A related question that is of central importance to Ayn Rand's philosophy is: By what means are we human beings to achieve our values? Her answer, of course, is that the fundamental method human beings must employ is rational thinking, or the mind—not faith, feelings, or even manual labor. Physical work is important and necessary to grow crops, build homes, and manufacture industrial products, but first and fundamentally some geniuses had to figure out how to do these things successfully. It was rational thinkers who discovered the new knowledge in mathematics, logic, philosophy, literature, the arts, physics, and other fields that enabled human beings to advance from caves and to modern industrial civilization. It was geniuses such as Aristotle, Galileo, Newton, Darwin, Pasteur, Edison, Shakespeare, Michelangelo, da Vinci, Beethoven, and others who identified, created, or formulated the principles of logic, the laws of motion, the theory of evolution, the germ theory of disease, and all the brilliant works of literature, painting, sculpture, and music that are of enduring value.

First, foremost, and fundamentally, the mind is the means by which men create the values that make possible the flourishing of human life on earth. This is true at the everyday level, as well. For example, an auto mechanic does not fix a car primarily by means of manual labor—but by thinking. In his case, to do an effective job, he must *understand* the workings of an internal combustion engine. This principle is also true of plumbers, carpenters, electricians, and other productive professionals whose constructive efforts depend on *knowledge* of their respective fields.

Even such back-breaking work as digging ditches with pick-axes and shovels (let alone derricks, dump trucks, and power drills) requires knowledge. For example, the ditch digger has a purpose in mind—irrigation, perhaps, or drainage; he must understand issues related to the project's length, depth, and time frame. Measuring and integrating all of these considerations require reason. Nonhuman animals could not do it. Even if an animal could be trained to grip tools, it could still not perform such tasks, because it could not understand the purpose of the work, its nature, or the measurements involved.

The role of reason in achieving human values is as fundamental in dealing with society as it is in dealing with nature. For example, in the interest of human life, people need to reason out their disagreements—and not permit them to degenerate into screaming irrationality, physical violence, or brutal, bloody warfare. Further, although love—an emotion—is certainly a vital component of friendships, romantic relationships, and child-rearing, reason nevertheless remains fundamental in these positive human interactions as well. For example, it is our rational mind—an honest, objective commitment to facts—not our feelings, that tells us if a person is trustworthy, responsible, and worth cultivating a relationship with over the course of a lifetime. It is possible to be blinded by love to an individual's faults—therefore, it is especially when our emotions are strongest that we most need a rational commitment to the facts of a given case.

Based on all of the points discussed in this chapter, Ayn Rand argued for the heroic capacity of human nature. Human beings can be heroes. They are not necessarily drug addicts, alcoholics, criminals, or whining losers. They can and often do struggle against terrible odds to reach glorious successes. How do they do this? By remaining true to their own values—come hell or high water—and to their own minds as the means of gaining those values.

HERO

The creators of values are the greatest heroes of the human race. Such rare individuals as Socrates, Galileo, Darwin, and other intellectual giants stood up against the masses and the social institutions of their times in support of positive ideas and life-giving theories that they knew to be true. They were committed to their own values, their own ideals, their own principles, their own minds—even at risk to their careers, their freedom, their very lives.

This could be any one of us. We need not be geniuses in order to be unwaveringly committed to our own beliefs, convictions, and values. When we are willing to face any and all obstacles in support of positive, healthy, life-promoting values, then we attain the status of heroes. Human nature is potentially noble.

What have we seen so far? It is morally right for a person to pursue his own values and happiness—and thinking (or rational achievement) is the fundamental means by which he does so. The person who is true to his own thinking, his own mind, and his own values in the face of any and all opposition is worthy of the designation "hero." Now the questions arise: What social condition is necessary to protect each individual's right to pursue his own values and happiness? Which political-economic system liberates each and every individual to guide his life by his own thinking?

Ayn Rand's answers are: the principle of individual rights, and the only political-economic system that puts it into practice— laissez-faire capitalism. If a human being is to gain values, meaning, and happiness, then he must be politically free to do so. *He must be acknowledged to possess an inalienable right to his own life, his own values, his own mind, and the pursuit of his own happiness.* This principle holds true of every individual regardless of gender, race, nationality, or other hereditary trait.

LAISSEZ-FAIRE CAPITALISM.

Ayn Rand's theory raises the question: Who or what are capable of violating an individual's right to his own life—and by what means? Her answer: Only other human beings can violate an individual's rights—and only by means of initiating force or fraud against him. But what does this mean, and why is it so?

For example, if an individual is alone on an island, a storm, a disease, or a natural disaster might prevent him from attaining his goals—or even end his life. But although his life is threatened by these natural circumstances, at least alone on the island *he remains free to take action against them*—free to em-

ploy his mind in an attempt to promote his life. At least on the deserted island, there are no evil men to rob, enslave, or murder him. This is why, as grim as life would be alone on the island, it would be vastly preferable to existence in Hitler's Germany or Stalin's Russia. At least alone, a man is free to take positive steps in support of his life. Under a dictatorship, he is not free to take such steps—he must forfeit his life to the government's whim.

Notice that other people violate an individual's rights only to the extent that they rob, beat, assault, deceive, or otherwise initiate direct or indirect force against him. As long as they do not use coercion against him, he remains free to act on his own thinking and judgment in pursuit of his own values and happiness. Even if other people try to *persuade* him to follow a self-destructive course of action, as long as they refrain from the use of force, he remains free to reject their proposal. Persuasion, no matter how toxic or irrational, cannot harm a man without his voluntary consent.

Consequently, human beings, in order to be able to strive toward their own goals and purposes in accordance with their own voluntary thinking, require an agency to protect their inalienable right to their own lives and minds. That agency is the government. A government is necessary to protect honest men from the initiation of force against them by criminals. *A proper government recognizes and protects an individual's right to his own life, mind, and pursuit of values.*

To this end, a written constitution is necessary, one including a bill of rights specifying the full range of an individual's incontestable and unassailable rights—for example, freedom of speech, of intellectual expression, of religion, and of private property. The United States Constitution, although not perfect, is a landmark document that helped to establish the freest country in history up to this time.

The only political-economic system to uphold and protect individual rights, Ayn Rand argued, is laissez-faire capitalism. Capitalism, she emphasized, is the system of individual rights,

including property rights, in which all property is privately owned. Under true capitalism, the government protects honest men from criminals—and the constitution prevents the government itself from becoming criminal. The key point is that the government is limited to the retaliatory use of force—and only against those who initiate its use. A proper government is then the protector of individual rights, not a violator of them.

A proper government is thereby limited to the performance of three functions. First, it must provide a police force and a criminal justice system to protect the innocent against criminals, i.e., (private force initiators). Second, it must provide a civil courts system to arbitrate legitimate disputes between and among honest men, to provide a legally binding forum within which to resolve such disputes, and to thereby prevent any individual from seeking resolution by the initiation of force against his neighbor. Third, it must also provide a volunteer military to defend the country against foreign aggressors. It is critical to observe that every proper function of government exists to *protect the innocent from any and all instances of the initiation of force.*

Capitalism is morally superior to all forms of statism for exactly this reason. Under statism—whether in the form of fascism, communism, military dictatorship, religious dictatorship, welfare state socialism, etc.—the government possesses the legal right to initiate force against its own citizens in a multitude of ways. For example, under various statist regimes, the government can impose taxes on honest men, redistribute wealth from productive people to unproductive ones, imprison or execute men for speaking out against the regime, draft them into the armed forces, ban a woman's right to abortion, steal a man's property by invoking the principle of eminent domain, and prevent an individual from developing his own property by imposing environmentalist laws and restrictions. The list goes on and on. Under any form of statism, the government can and does initiate force endlessly against its own citizens.

Only laissez-faire capitalism bans the government's initiation of force, and legally restricts it to a retaliatory use. The practical consequences are superlative. In the span of a few short centuries, the capitalist nations of Western Europe, North America, Hong Kong, South Korea, Singapore, Taiwan, and Japan have risen out of the atrocious poverty so dominant throughout human history and up to standards of living undreamed of by the people of previous eras. This is extraordinary—but not surprising in light of Ayn Rand's philosophy.

Remember, the mind is mankind's primary means of creating the ideas, theories, goods and services upon which human survival and prosperity depend. But the mind requires freedom. Whip-driven manual labor (or slavery) exists under statism—and plenty of it—but is not capable of creating abundance. The great independent thinkers in every field require political-economic freedom to make the breakthroughs necessary for progress.

Under capitalism, with the principle of individual rights upheld and protected, the great thinkers are free to make creative breakthroughs, to overturn ideas previously dominant in many fields, and to challenge intellectually any and all authority, including both church and state. For example, witness the explosive advances in applied science and technology in the capitalist nations. Thomas Edison created the electric lighting system; the Wright brothers invented the airplane; Henry Ford revolutionized transportation by mass producing the automobile; and George Eastman similarly revolutionized photography by inventing the Kodak camera.

In the free countries of the West, intellectual progress flourishes. Scientists continue to develop new theories, and medical researchers continue to develop new cures and procedures. In every major city, writers, musicians, and artists are able to flourish within the publishing industry, music industry, and art world, respectively. Even anti-capitalist artists of every variety, who scorn the "crass vulgarity" of moneymaking, are left free to pursue their own noncommercial dreams.

In the absence of free intellectual expression as an application of a broader principle of individual rights, what would happen to creative geniuses who disagree with political or religious authority? What would have happened to Darwin, for example, had he expressed his theories during the Middle Ages or under a religious fundamentalist regime? What happened to independent minds under the Nazis or Communists? They were imprisoned, enslaved, or killed. What happens to freethinkers under any type of dictatorship? They are often incarcerated as political prisoners or murdered.

Observe that the medieval Catholic Church, the leaders of modern Islamism, the Nazis, and the Communists, despite many differences, share two important characteristics in common: First, they impose brutal dictatorships that require blind obedience—and execute the freethinking minds who dissent. Second, they lead their countries to inhuman squalor and ruinous warfare. The first point leads directly to the second: suppressing the mind leads inevitably to destruction in numerous forms.

Individual rights and capitalism are necessary for progress in every creative field and the flourishing of human life on earth. The more statist a society, the more power it has to control the minds and lives of its individual citizens—and the more surely and deeply it regresses into poverty and misery. In order to reach the prosperity of the modern Western countries, a society must respect the rights of every individual to his own mind and life. Capitalism is the sole social system capable of supporting freedom and creating prosperity.

Chapter 6
The Deeper Theories
of Objectivism

Now, you might say:

> NOW, I GET ALL OF THIS STUFF ABOUT EGOISM—ABOUT GAINING THE VALUES WE LOVE, AND DOING IT BY HARD WORK AND HONEST EFFORT, NOT BY LYING, CHEATING, STEALING, OR VICTIMIZING INNOCENT PEOPLE.

> AND I UNDERSTAND THAT IT IS THROUGH REASON AND THE USE OF OUR MINDS THAT WE SURVIVE AND PROSPER ON EARTH – NOT BY DECEPTION, DUPLICITY, BRUTE FORCE, CONQUEST, OR PLUNDER.

> I SEE THE NEED OF INDIVIDUAL RIGHTS, LIMITED GOVERNMENT, AND CAPITALISM.

> BUT WHY THE NAME "OBJECTIVISM?" WHY DID AYN RAND CHOOSE SUCH AN UNUSUAL AND COMPLEX NAME FOR HER PHILOSOPHY?

That's a good question—and Ayn Rand had a good answer for it. The short answer is she believed that both knowledge and values are objective. What in blazes does that mean? An idea is objective if it is based in facts and there is hard evidence or data to back it up; it is not just an individual's personal whim, desire, or belief. So to say that knowledge and values are objective is to say that human knowledge and judgments of right and wrong can and should be based in facts—not just in the feelings or the faith of a person or group. Let's examine these elements one at a time.

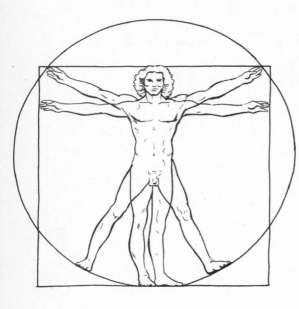

Knowledge, according to Ayn Rand and a long line of philosophers and scientists, originates in sense experience and observation—in that which we can see, touch, hear, etc. To put it simply, all knowledge originates in observational facts. Such a theory in *epistemology*—just a big word for the study of how human beings gain knowledge—denies that human knowledge is based in religious faith or a person's feelings.

By contrast, in religion, we are supposed to start with a book that is held to be the word of God—whether the Bible, the Koran, or some other religious text—and then accept its teachings without question or criticism. According to this method, therefore, some people believe that women are turned to pillars of salt, men walk on water, the sun stands still in the sky, and other similar beliefs.

In the modern Western world, religion is not as influential as it was during the Middle Ages or in large parts of the Islamic world today. However, many people today believe that you must simply "trust your heart." This means that you should basically follow your emotions; if you deeply and sincerely feel something is true or good, then it is true or good for you. In other words, a person's feelings are the only evidence he requires to determine if a claim is true or false, right or wrong. This means, for example, that if I believe in astrology, numerology, tarot card reading, or alien landings, then such beliefs are true for me. Similarly, if I feel that drug use, indiscriminate sex, or even violence is right, then such actions are right for me. This theory is known as *emotionalism*. Ayn Rand rejected such beliefs as irrational. Without facts to back them up, they are merely arbitrary beliefs with no hard, supporting evidence.

Now let's contrast emotionalist beliefs with fact-based claims from both common sense and science. For example, many mothers tell their children that eating fruits and vegetables is good for them, while eating candy or other sweets (at least in excess) is not. Notice the foundations of such simple claims. According to common sense, people who get vitamins and minerals from nutritious foods will likely get sick less often and have more energy—especially if they combine a balanced diet with sufficient sleep, water, and exercise. On the other hand, those who eat too many sweets will likely experience "sugar highs" followed by significant drops in energy. They will also be prone to stomach aches—and, in time, will probably need more dental work.

Further, advances in biology, nutrition, and medicine help explain the underlying causes of such everyday experiences. Today, we have scientific backing for Mom's claims. We know enough biochemistry to explain the positive physical effects of non-fatty protein and vitamin- and mineral-rich fruits and vegetables—and the harmful physical effects of a diet overloaded with sugar. In short, Mom's common-sense claims regarding such matters are backed by an impressive body of factual evidence.

These are simple examples, to be sure. Nevertheless, they are valid examples of *objectivity*—of claims that are based in facts, not in faith or feelings. The upshot of this is that any theory—whether in science, philosophy, or any other field—*if it is true*, can and must be validated by the support of a wealth of factual information. In science, for example, Newton's law of universal gravitation has a ton of hard evidence to support it. In millions of instances, the attraction between bodies is demonstrated. If a person throws a ball in the air, it comes back to earth. If something falls off a table, it drops to the floor. If someone slips on the stairs or a hillside, he plummets downward. All flying organisms or objects—from birds to planes to rockets—demonstrate the need to generate a force superior to gravitational pull in order to be propelled through the air. If that force is annulled, the object ceases to fly and crashes to the earth.

Philosophical truths, like scientific ones, are supported by factual evidence. For example, take Ayn Rand's claims that the rational mind is the source of human progress and prosperity—and that the creative mind requires political-economic freedom. In case after case, such claims are demonstrated to be true.

Take the first, more fundamental point first. The advances in agricultural science and technology necessary to grow an abundance of food; the inventions of electric light, airplanes, personal computers, and the Internet; the progress in medical research and the development of new

OWW!!!

pharmaceuticals; the identification of deeper scientific truths, such as the theory of evolution; creative work in the arts; pioneering developments in philosophy; and countless other examples in the modern world provide a plethora of facts demonstrating the life-giving power of the mind.

Similarly, regarding the point about political-economic freedom, when the freethinking mind is suppressed by overbearing religious authority, as in medieval Europe, a dark age ensues. When the mind is repressed by dictatorial governments—as under the Communists in Cuba, North Korea, and the former Soviet Union—the result is stagnation, grinding poverty, and abysmal collapse. But when the mind is free, as in the modern Western nations and the Hong Kong, South Korea, Singapore, Taiwan, and Japan, advances are made in all of the creative fields described above—and human living standards and life expectancies soar to historically unprecedented heights. A wealth of factual data supports the claim that political-economic freedom is an enormous boon to human life.

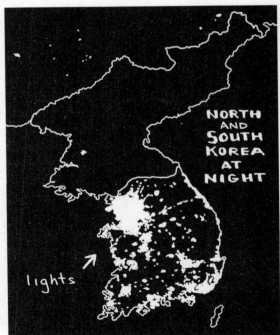

NORTH AND SOUTH KOREA AT NIGHT

lights

These are but a few of the points Ayn Rand had in mind when she described human knowledge as "objective." She also asserted that our moral judgments—our claims regarding right and wrong, good and evil—can and should be grounded in objective fact rather than in the feelings or the faith of any person or group.

But how can that be? After all, in our day, it is widely held that every society develops its own morals and ideas of right and wrong—that these differ from society to society—and that it is impossible to judge one society's beliefs superior to another. This popular theory is known as "moral relativism." Today, it is sometimes referred to as "multiculturalism."

Further, religion is still popular in many parts of the world—and religion certainly has no factual basis to its moral claims. For example, there is no evidence to support the claim that human beings are born in sin, that God is morally pure (or even that He exists), that God is the source of biblical commandments, and that virtue lies in unquestioning obedience to these commands. These are purely matters of faith. So how could Ayn Rand have claimed that a proper ethics is grounded entirely in facts and reason? Was she crazy? Did she need to go back to the drawing board to rethink her theories?

 Her answer to such questions were—and remain—revolutionary, but can be explained clearly and simply. Let's start with an example: Suppose a man works honestly and productively, and supports himself by his own effort, without lying, cheating, or duplicity. Most people would undoubtedly agree that such a course of action is good. But what makes it good? Is it good simply because most people in our society deem it so? Or is it good because God commands it of us? Or, alternatively, is it good because some fact(s) of reality—some law of nature—requires it if human beings are to live well on earth?

Ayn Rand's answer was, of course, the latter. Why? For one thing, she raised the question in a new form. She did not ask: Is there some connection between facts and human judgments of good and evil? Rather, she asked: What basic fact of reality gives rise to man's need of making such assessments of right and wrong, good and evil? In effect, given human nature, we clearly have some inherent need to evaluate good and evil—but what is it?

Let's go back to earlier examples and examine them more closely—examples that go beyond human beings and human nature. Let's look more broadly at living beings as such—and then come back to man. Observe, for example, that plants dig their roots into the soil in order to gain chemical nutrients, and grow their leaves toward the sun in order to gain its light. Why do they do this? Because their lives depend on such activities. In order to sustain their existence, they must achieve certain goals. In the absence of fertile soil, sunlight, and rainwater, they will die. Notice that they have no choice in what will benefit their lives—or what will harm them. Such issues are determined entirely by their nature, by the requirements of their survival, and by the laws of reality. What is beneficial or harmful to them is strictly and solely a matter of fact.

The same is true of animals. Different species hunt food, build nests, burrow holes in the ground, and migrate with the seasons, all in service of their lives. They take action seeking the food, shelter, and warmer weather that their lives depend on. Again, it is important to observe that animals, like plants, have no choice in the matter of what benefits and harms them. Such issues are entirely governed by the inflexible, unalterable laws of nature.

The same principle applies to human beings. In order to flourish on earth—indeed, in order merely to survive—men need to grow crops, domesticate livestock, build houses, perform medical research, cure diseases, and study philosophy, logic, mathematics, and the sciences in order to carry out such constructive activities. Again, human beings have no choice or options regarding the basic requirements of their lives.

Unlike plants or animals, however, people must choose to pursue what is in their self-interest; it is not automatic or instinctual on their part. They can choose poison over food, ignorance over education, and faith over reason, secular philosophy, and science—but they cannot avoid the consequences of those choices. For example, they can flout nature's laws by choosing booze, drugs, and indiscriminate sex over clean, healthy living—but their health and life expectancies will suffer as a result.

Such points form the foundation of a fact-based, rational, objective ethics. The good, for any species, is that which furthers its life. The evil is that which harms it. For man, who is a rational animal surviving by the functioning of his mind, the good is all that which furthers the life of a rational being—and the evil is all that which harms or destroys it.

Take several examples. Whether or not children like vegetables, vegetables are *in fact* nutritious and health-supporting. Whether or not some people want an education, an education *in fact* trains a person's mind (or survival instrument), and is therefore of vital importance to human survival. Regardless of how many people voluntarily follow the Nazis, Communists, or Islamists, the protections of individual rights, political-economic freedom, and capitalism are *in fact* necessary to protect the rational mind, to safeguard an individual's inalienable right to his own life, and thereby to ensure that individuals can survive and prosper on earth.

In Ayn Rand's terms, the factual requirements of human life form the standard by which to measure something as good or evil. If some thing, person, or action promotes human life and well-being, then it is good. If it harms or destroys human life, then it is evil.

Ayn Rand supported reason, instead of faith and emotionalism. Because it is mankind's survival instrument, it is therefore good. She upheld capitalism over every form of statism because it is the only system to liberate a human being to employ his own mind in support of his own life. It is the only system that enhances human life—and is therefore good without qualification. This is why she glorifies productive careers, romantic love, and value-based friendships in her novels —because each, in its own way, is a requirement of a fulfilled and happy life, and each therefore is good.

Why is it good for an individual to work hard to support himself by honest effort? Because we do not reside in a Garden of Eden—because the things that our lives require do not exist readymade in nature. Those life-promoting values must be created by human effort. Productive work supports human life and is therefore good.

This is what Ayn Rand meant when she described ethics, morality, value judgments, and appraisals of good and evil as objective. Ethics is not a matter of human desire, whim, or emotion; nor is it a matter of blind faith in a fantasy dimension of the supernatural. Rather, it is a science whose purpose is to guide human beings to successful, prosperous, joyous lives on earth.

Because she held that knowledge and evaluations of right and wrong are objective, she chose the name of Objectivism for her philosophy.

Chapter 7
Objectivism and the Objectivist Movement Today

The publication of *Atlas Shrugged* in 1957 launched the Objectivist movement. The goal of Ayn Rand's philosophy was not to instigate political revolution—as was the goal of Marx's theory a hundred years earlier. The goal was rather to promote a cultural renaissance—a much broader, more sweeping, and infinitely more peaceful purpose.

In Ayn Rand's time, the modern world continued to advance in science, medicine, and technology, much as it does today. This was good, but in Ayn Rand's judgment the state of the humanities was deplorable. Literature was forsaking hero- and plot-driven stories for rambling tales about losers of every imaginable variety (or "antiheroes"). Music became decreasingly melodic and increasingly dissonant—more like noise than music. Art became dominated by non-representational paintings—blobs smeared on a canvas or simply streaks of color representing nothing. The content taught in schools had become so diluted that it was fair to say that the educational system was on the verge of collapse. Politics became overwhelmingly anti-individual rights as the United States moved away from political-economic freedom and capitalism and deeper into a statist hybrid combining elements of a European-style socialist state with elements of religious theocracy.

Ayn Rand sought to reverse these ominous trends. Her books and ideas were designed to promote heroism and plot in literature, melody in music, beauty in art, rigorous academic content in education, and individual rights and political-economic freedom in politics. Her books sparked intense controversy—and founded a movement.

In the past fifty years, Objectivism has slowly, tortuously, but inexorably worked its way into the mainstream of American culture. Here are but several examples: A film documentary of Rand's life was nominated for an Academy Award entitled *Ayn Rand: A*

Sense of Life. An endless stream of books about her theories are being published, most notably Dr. Leonard Peikoff's *Objectivism: The Philosophy of Ayn Rand.* Think tanks and research fellowships affiliated with such major universities as the University of Pittsburgh and the University of Texas, among others, have been set up specifically to study Ayn Rand's books and theories.

There is an Ayn Rand Society within the American Philosophical Association, the professional organization of philosophers, designed to foster a greater understanding of her work by contemporary philosophers. A growing number of young Objectivist intellectuals are receiving PhDs in various academic fields and then going on to teach in the universities. High school essay contests on the subject of her novels draw tens of thousands of entries each year. Objectivist intellectuals now appear regularly on TV and radio, especially Dr. Yaron Brook, executive director of the Ayn Rand Institute. Op-ed essays written by Objectivist writers have appeared in the nation's major newspapers. The United States Postal Service even issued an Ayn Rand commemorative stamp. As early as 1991, a combined survey of readers conducted by the Library of Congress and the Book-of-the-Month Club showed *Atlas Shrugged* as the second most influential book in America—second only to the Bible (which has had something of a head start).

The establishment of the Ayn Rand Institute (ARI) in California in 1985 was a major step forward in promoting Objectivism. Now there was an organization of Objectivist intellectuals dedicated to infusing the American educational system with Ayn Rand's books and ideas. To that end, ARI sponsors the aforementioned high school essay contests, puts hundreds of thousands of copies of Ayn Rand's novels into the hands of high school English teachers in the United States and Canada for use in their courses, and sends its intellectuals into high school classes to discuss those books and ideas.

ARI also operates the Objectivist Academic Center (OAC), which offers courses—sometimes for college credit—in Objectivism, writing, and other intellectual topics to young Objectivist thinkers coming up through the universities. The organization also offers support to Objectivist students on college campuses who form clubs to study Ayn Rand's philosophy, sending them literature and video lectures. Further, the OAC manages a speaker's bureau of intellectuals who provide live talks on philosophy, literature, and politics. Recently, ARI opened the Ayn Rand Center for Individual Rights in Washington, DC, to campaign for political-economic freedom in the nation's capital. Other smaller and less prominent organizations influenced by Ayn Rand also work to promote her books and ideas in the educational system and in Western culture more broadly.

There exists intense opposition, of course. Most current professors, teachers, critics, and other experts in the humanities regard Ayn Rand as either a nobody—an in-significant pest or a deranged madwoman—or an evil influence in the lives of her unsuspecting readers. For example, they often claim that *Atlas Shrugged*, as a novel, is too long, too preachy, less a literary work than a mere soapbox from which to spout ideas, or just an encyclopedia filled with false and dangerous philosophy. Interestingly, the English professors in America's colleges and universities—the leading experts in

the field of literature—as a general rule show no interest whatsoever in Ayn Rand's novels. They generally ignore them, and, if roused to comment on them at all, often denounce them.

This situation is not so extreme in the philosophy departments of our universities. As already noted, a growing number of professors and universities are showing interest in teaching and researching Ayn Rand's philosophical ideas. Still, the overwhelming majority of America's philosophy professors are either indifferent or hostile to Rand's theories. Generally, they regard her as either a cult figure or a "pop philosopher" offering half-baked ideas to people with no training in rigorous philosophy. Either way, she is regarded as a minor figure unworthy of serious study.

But as singer-songwriter Bob Dylan once noted (albeit in a completely different context with a completely different meaning), "the times they are a-changin'." In fact, societies always change, even if sometimes at a glacially slow pace. Consider, for example, the repeal of the Jim Crow laws and the desegregation of the American South. Nothing in the universe, whether man-made or existing in nature, remains static or stagnant. As thousands of young people every year study *The Fountainhead* and *Atlas Shrugged* in their eleventh- and twelfth-grade Advanced Placement English courses, a number of these bright, young minds are highly likely to become fascinated with Ayn Rand's books and theories, seek careers in the humanities, and become teachers, professors, or writers who will, in the fullness of time, introduce Ayn Rand's ideas to many of their own students and readers. The educational system is always the conduit between the ideas of a revolutionary thinker and a mass audience—and it is no different in Ayn Rand's case.

Over the past fifty to sixty years, Ayn Rand's novels have been deeply woven into the fabric of American society and the intellectual culture into which bright, young people are born. An increasing number of the country's future teachers and intellectuals are reading them and being positively influenced by them. As the years go by, the older generation of American teachers and intellectuals who are indifferent or hostile to Ayn Rand's ideas will age and retire. They will be replaced by younger men and women, many of whom recognize the positive value of her ideas. This is how original ideas, no matter how revolutionary or controversial, are eventually introduced into a cultural mainstream—and this is how societies are changed. As economist Henry Hazlitt once noted, "Reason is slow yeast but it brews incessantly."

What is the prognosis in the twenty-first century for the Objectivist movement? Recent 2007 and 2008 surveys by pollster John Zogby show that 8 percent of respondents and more than 17 percent of American college graduates have read *Atlas Shrugged*. Even with the overall decline of the American educational system, these numbers will only increase over the coming years. And however slow and tortuous the process might be, American civilization and the world beyond will be increasingly impacted by Ayn Rand's message.

About the Author & Illustrator:

Andrew Bernstein, Ph.D. has published on a wide variety of philosophical and literary issues based on Ayn Rand's philosophies including Objectivism In One Lesson: An Introduction to the Philosophy Of Ayn Rand. His book, The Capitalist Manifesto: The Historic, Economic, and Philosophic Case for Laissez-Faire, was published in 2005. Dr. Bernstein is a Visiting Professor of Philosophy at Marist College; he also teaches at SUNY Purchase (which selected him Outstanding Teacher for 2004)—and formerly at Pace University, and Marymount College (which selected him Outstanding Teacher for 1995). He has taught at Hunter College, Long Island University, and many other New York-area colleges. He lectures frequently at philosophy conferences all over the United States; additionally in Canada, England, Belgium, Norway, Hong Kong and Bermuda.

Owen Brozman is an artist who lives and works in New York City. He has an MFA in Illustration from the School of Visual Arts and a BFA in Painting from Boston University. Publications and clients include 3x3 Illustration Annual, Creative Quarterly Journal, Paramount Vantage, Playboy Magazine, Scholastic, and Ninja Tune Records.

You can see more of Owen's work at www.owenbrozman.com

THE FOR BEGINNERS® SERIES

AFRICAN HISTORY FOR BEGINNERS: ISBN 978-1-934389-18-8

ANARCHISM FOR BEGINNERS: ISBN 978-1-934389-32-4

ARABS & ISRAEL FOR BEGINNERS: ISBN 978-1-934389-16-4

ASTRONOMY FOR BEGINNERS: ISBN 978-1-934389-25-6

BARACK OBAMA FOR BEGINNERS, AN ESSENTIAL GUIDE: ISBN 978-1-934389-44-7

BLACK HISTORY FOR BEGINNERS: ISBN 978-1-934389-19-5

THE BLACK HOLOCAUST FOR BEGINNERS: ISBN 978-1-934389-03-4

BLACK WOMEN FOR BEGINNERS: ISBN 978-1-934389-20-1

CHOMSKY FOR BEGINNERS: ISBN 978-1-934389-17-1

DADA & SURREALISM FOR BEGINNERS: ISBN 978-1-934389-00-3

DECONSTRUCTION FOR BEGINNERS: ISBN 978-1-934389-26-3

DEMOCRACY FOR BEGINNERS: ISBN 978-1-934389-36-2

DERRIDA FOR BEGINNERS: ISBN 978-1-934389-11-9

EASTERN PHILOSOPHY FOR BEGINNERS: ISBN 978-1-934389-07-2

EXISTENTIALISM FOR BEGINNERS: ISBN 978-1-934389-21-8

FOUCAULT FOR BEGINNERS: ISBN 978-1-934389-12-6

GLOBAL WARMING FOR BEGINNERS: ISBN 978-1-934389-27-0

HEIDEGGER FOR BEGINNERS: ISBN 978-1-934389-13-3

ISLAM FOR BEGINNERS: ISBN 978-1-934389-01-0

KIERKEGAARD FOR BEGINNERS: ISBN 978-1-934389-14-0

LACAN FOR BEGINNERS: ISBN 978-1-934389-39-3

LINGUISTICS FOR BEGINNERS: ISBN 978-1-934389-28-7

MALCOLM X FOR BEGINNERS:

NIETZSCHE FOR BEGINNERS:

THE OLYMPICS FOR BEGINNERS:

PHILOSOPHY FOR BEGINNERS:

PLATO FOR BEGINNERS:

POSTMODERNISM FOR BEGINNERS:

SARTRE FOR BEGINNERS:

SHAKESPEARE FOR BEGINNERS:

STRUCTURALISM & POSTSTRUCTURALISM FOR BEGINNERS

ZEN FOR BEGINNERS:

ZINN FOR BEGINNERS:

www.forbeginnersbooks